D0811167

Irish
SUPERSTITIONS

Irish

SUPERSTITIONS

PADRAIC O'FARRELL

MERCIER PRESS

MERCIER PRESS
Cork
www.mercierpress.ie

© Estate of Padraic O'Farrell, 2019
First published as *Superstitions of the Irish Country People*
in 1978. Revised enlarged edition, 1982. This edition first
published in 2019.

ISBN: 978 1 78117 693 1

A CIP record for this title is available from the British
Library

Printed and bound in the EU.

CONTENTS

INTRODUCTION

Custom, then, is the great guide of human life.

So wrote the Scottish philosopher, David Hume, in his *An Enquiry Concerning Human Understanding* written in 1748. While the opening paragraphs of a book on the superstitions and customs of Irish country people is no place to become embroiled in the theories of an eminent scholar, the quotation is worth pondering upon in the context with which we are concerned.

Human life has been defined in many ways. There have been vast areas of disagreement among its definers. Living in its fullest sense is still dear to Irish countryfolk and is reflected in their customs.

As the brash commercialism and the vulgar

opulence of modern living engulf thoughtful-
ness, refinement, gentility and Christianity,
more and more of the old customs of our people
are dying out.

But does one ever really know if a custom or
superstition has died out? Can one be certain
that the farmer whose pre-dawn path has been
crossed by a hare does not fear the consequences
for the remainder of the day – or that he does
not purposely avoid the taking of a lighted coal
from the fire on May Day for fear of taking the
blessing from the house? How can one be sure
that the jean-clad youth who lounges against
the door of the village hall is not regretting
his rash daring in saying 'God bless it' of a cat
before he embarked on his amorous pursuits for
the evening? After all, hadn't his mother told
him of the Kerry priest who had forbidden this
because of the demon cat keeping him from a

deathbed by his plaintive singing of *Cailín Deas Crúite na mBó*?

Last summer, I ribbed an aunt who had treated my son's warts with a fresh-cut potato and then buried the half-potato so used in the garden. I told her that the half-potato must have grown and that the whole family must have eaten of the crop for weren't we all then displaying ugly volcanic eruptions. She smiled and set about splitting more potatoes – despite protests from an economic housewife who was paying dearly for her golden wonders at the time …

As I begin the first chapter of this book my family are rid of their warts while I notice a scraping sound on my paper. The noise is occasioned by my little finger drearily dragging a truly enormous appendage along the page. It looks like *Meascán Mhéabha* atop Sligo's Knocknarea.

So stay with me for these few pages and perhaps my scraping finger will scour the surface of this cairn of fascinating lore and whet the reader's appetite for more. Stay with me anyhow – if only to discover how the wart looks when my mission has been completed.

1

PEOPLE

Ask any Irish person if he or she knows of an old superstition and no matter how ill-versed in our lore, he or she will almost certainly declare that a red-haired woman is unlucky. Said to be typically Irish, red-haired women were nonetheless treated with great suspicion and if a man met one as he was going to work he would almost certainly forget all about his labours and go home.

Certain other individuals often got the name of being unlucky to meet. This usually came about through their having been associated with a tragedy. Some families carried a stigma because of this.

It was considered unlucky to meet a bare-footed man, and if somebody happened on a man on his way to work and asked where he was going, the man would call off his errand in order to avoid catastrophe.

An evil spirit might enter your inner self and live with you if your yawn was not followed by the making of the Sign of the Cross over your mouth.

For the same reason, whistling was considered unlucky under certain circumstances. Fishermen did not whistle on board, nor did actors in their dressing rooms, and a whistling woman, not to mind a whistling mother-in-law, was never welcome.

Nobody ever crossed the path of a horse team and plough, nor would anybody, however roguish, dream of stealing a plough. And while on the subject of honesty, stealing from a smith, or blacksmith, was not just dishonest – it was downright dangerous.

Walking around a card table could change a player's luck if the walking was conducted in a sunwise direction … provided the sun was shining on the opponent's hand!

A crooked pin in a lapel was lucky too.

A smoker always smoked indoors for a while before leaving the house. To do otherwise was considered unlucky.

A good wash in the morning dew on May Day was said to work wonders for a maiden's beauty.

Dreams were treated with a certain amount of awe among country people and some individuals were said to be able to interpret dreams. Dreams were never revealed before the dreamer's fast was broken and, if possible, a girl called Mary would be the first to hear a dream.

Dreams involving horses were lucky, while dreams about priests or a wedding were unlucky.

To dream of being kissed by a woman meant deceit, but if the dreamer saw a hearse drawn by plumed horses it might well foretell a wedding for himself.

The new moon was treated with great suspicion and if it was first seen through glass it would be most unlucky. Pocket money being turned and bowing to the crescent seven times helped allay mishaps.

Red-haired men had their share of trouble as well as women of the same hue. Some claimed that all this obsession with red hair stemmed from the fact that Judas, who betrayed Jesus, had red hair.

A childless woman who stared at another's child was to be treated with great caution. The 'evil eye' could spirit away an infant and a suspicious-looking childless woman might well be a talent spotter for a childless spirit.

Pointed instruments, hooks, gaffs or knives were never handed to others without first being stuck into something wooden. It was thought that friendships could be severed if this precaution was not observed. This probably had some connection with the reluctance to give a knife or a sharp instrument as a gift. I treated this idea with contempt as a boy and often begged my sisters for a strong penknife – and many family friendships were severed as a result!

It was thought unlucky to walk under a ladder – even before vaudeville latched on to the dropping of paint on persons doing so.

Breaking a mirror brought seven years of bad luck, while two people washing their hands in the same basin at the same time courted disaster.

Of course, the throwing of a pinch of salt

over the shoulder was an antidote for all these misfortunes.

Widows were often treated with respect because of the dreaded 'widow's curse' which some of them were said to have the power of bringing down. A young widow, a travelling woman, and her sick child were pitied by some tenants, who built them a cabin on their landlord's land to protect them from the weather. They were evicted by the landlord and their cabin was burned. When the child died from exposure, the widow brought down the curse that for seven generations none of the landlord's male heirs would die under normal circumstances. Suicides, sea disasters, hunting accidents and shootings claimed all the landlord's descendants for seven generations.

A drink of the distilled juice of deadly nightshade would make a person believe anything he was told, while the Devil would grant a man anything if he was called upon from beneath a double-ended briar.

Seeing a churning and not helping was unlucky. So was extinguishing a light when people were eating their supper.

Every day had one hour in which a wish would be granted and in which a person had the power to see spirits. Only by trial and error could that period be known.

It was unlucky to kill an old crane or a swan because they were bewitched old people.

A tinker once blinded the Devil and therefore no tinker will ever go to Hell. Nonetheless, the tinkers tell of a great clock that ticks forever in Hell.

Yet the tinkers were not very superstitious. They had the very philosophical saying: There is no day unlucky, only the day you cannot get enough to eat.

Tinkers used to 'trade in' carts or horses long before that became an accepted form of dealing in transport. They even had a type of pawn system whereby one could get a 'pound boot' by depositing a cart or other attractive items for further redemption.

As we leave this section, let me tell you how to become invisible:

With a black-handled knife make three cuts in the heart of a black raven. Put one black bean in each cut and sew the heart. When the beans grow put one in your mouth and say:

By virtue of Satan's heart
And by the strength of my great art,
I desire to be invisible.

… My daughter runs past my window screaming

that the typewriter keys are hopping up and down on their own!

2

SPIRITS AND FAIRIES

Fairies, spirits, the 'wee folk', leprechauns – their nomenclature depends more on the listener than the narrator, for few Irish country people can bear to deny the foreigner his simple pleasure in believing that around the next corner or in the very next clump of thistles there may well be lurking someone who will lead him to the crock of gold at the end of the rainbow. But the smile of the countryman could also change to a grim determined stare if, for instance, the stranger was outlining the course of a large earthmover and that giant hulk faced a 'Fairy Fort'.

The relationship between country people and

their spirits has always been an unstable affair. There has sometimes been an unwillingness to admit acceptance of the existence of fairies or spirits, but there has always been a healthy respect for the possibility.

Certain families were said to have been 'followed by the Banshee'. This was particularly true of families with musical talents. The Banshee was said to cry near the home of one who was about to die and she was said to follow a family to the ends of the earth. She had a particular attachment to the branches of the O'Grady family. A battered comb found in a ditch or a hedge was said to be hers, for she paid great attention to her coiffure.

Under the blanket term 'fairies' let us look at a few established customs that had to do with them.

Crumbs that dropped from the table were

often left for 'them' and if one suspected that they were up to some devilment, then a hat, a wedding dress or a left shoe could be thrown in their direction.

The 'changeling' has figured in folklore to an amazing extent. Old women suddenly appear in households and help with the baby's toilet as the mother sits with her eyes glued to her child, for she knows that if she takes her eyes away the baby will be 'changed'.

Fairy 'passes' were simply routes used by the 'wee folk' as they went about their business. Mortals seldom knew of their whereabouts – unless they decided to build a house or a shed on fairy land. If they did, a representative of the fairies might appear and ask the mortal to change his site – for a consideration, usually prosperity in the future.

Less lucky mortals might go ahead with the

building without this planning permission and have it demolished by the power of the fairies. It was accepted that building between two forts was not to be recommended as, obviously, the fairies would be passing from one fort to the other. In cases of doubt, the foundations would be dug and left for a few nights to see if the fairies would fill them in.

A case history from County Longford tells how a returned American insisted on building a new house between two forts, against all advice. All the neighbours were invited in for a 'house warmer', another country custom, when a party was held in the new premises. Good spirits prevailed until twelve o'clock, then the bad spirits had their fling in earnest. They flung pots, cups, saucers and pans around the house, and in no time the roof fell in. People fell, tripped and got buffeted by some unknown force. The piper's mouth went around to the back of his head and the owner of the house sprouted a horn on his forehead. In the morning, there was no sign of the new house and the owner hurried back to America.

It was commonly believed that the evil fairies were the *Tuatha de Danann*, who ruled Ireland before being conquered by the Milesians, and that they lived in caves around our shores. They stabled their fine steeds in the caves and a fisherman who chanced upon them lyrically described them:

Seven score steed, each with a jewel on his forehead like a star and seven score horsemen, all sons of kings in their green mantles fringed with gold and golden helmets on their heads and golden greaves on the limbs and each knight having in his hand a golden spear.

Fairies, whether on land or on sea, talked like mortals. They farmed and kept livestock too. They had marvellous parties on the hillsides and on the beaches, and they were always on the lookout for a handsome maid to hie away to a soirée on the clifftop.

Some people claimed that a person born in the morning could never see a fairy but that one born after midday could perhaps see one in the swirling eddy of dust they caused as they danced.

Missing potatoes were not searched for in the Irish countryside because the culprits were better left alone, and pails of water were often left for them to bathe in.

Some people believe that hordes of the 'wee folk' or 'good people' live under the earth, under *sceacha* (bushes) and are under the influence of the devil and other sinister beings. They emerge on particular feast days, or when disturbed, to cause unrest among mortals and to play pranks on them.

There are two types of fairies: 'trooping fairies' and 'solitary fairies'. We must suppose that the latter are slightly paranoid, anti-social and more likely to do something underhand like stealing an infant, than something generous like bringing a lucky wayfarer into the heart of some hill to be wined and feasted and, perhaps, introduced to the Queen of the Sidhe herself, within her fine palace. There she might well reward her visitor with regal lasciviousness, for strict moral standards were not part of the code of behaviour among Irish fairy royalty.

Like their compatriot mortals, fairies loved horse racing and beautiful women. A society reporter once described Queen Oonagh, wife of Fionvarra of the Connaught fairies, as having fine blonde hair trailing behind her and wearing a dew-drop gown which shimmered like soft mist upon her beautifully formed body. In spite of this, the gossip columnists described Fionvarra as a bit of a fairy-about-town, who dashed about on his six-inch-tall steed which breathed flames through red nostrils. Hitching his charger to a hawthorn, the master sought out young maidens for his pleasure.

Fairy raths or *liosanna* were systematically erected. While standing on top of one, others should be within sight to the left and to the right. A shy, wan, sickly man could be imbued with the fiery temperament of a *Tuatha de Danann* warrior by sleeping on a fairy rath.

The only fairy who could not be contended with through the use of spells was the foolish fairy. Madge Moran, Moll Anthony, Biddy Early and other illustrious women with postgraduate experience in anti-fairy warfare were powerless against the fairy fool who wandered around during midsummer. This fellow dressed in a tall hat and little else. He hurled stones at people, tripped them, tugged at them. He could drive a mortal insane.

We made a passing reference to fairy feasting, but these people, it must be stressed, went in for high-class cuisine. Their banqueting tables were laid with golden goblets and platters on tablecloths woven from spider web and rosepetals, and embroidered with ferns. They ate food stolen from mortals, but often frightened mortal guests by showing them their kitchens, where chickens roasting on a spit appeared as human babies to the mortal eye. They drank mead or nectar and were extremely hospitable. A mortal who accepted their invitation to dinner, however, had to bring along his own pinch of salt to season the fare, for his hosts didn't supply it. Yet without it the mortal could finish up 'in the fairies' – possessed by them.

Fairies were good to mortals who observed the superstitions, which called for leaving them food, not throwing out water without shouting a warning to them, and so on. They even parted with some of their golden apples, waters of wisdom, swords of knowledge and bottles of wine or loaves that never run out to such considerate people. This was, of course, after shark-infested seas were sailed and walls guarded by huge dogs climbed, teeth pulled from giant cats, and castles pulled down from the clouds.

Fairies hated the disbeliever most of all and if made angry they would leave him with a stammer or with feet which couldn't stop dancing or with a fine hump on his back.

An invitation to a fairy party was given in

verse to Edain, wife of the King of Munster, by a stranger who beat her husband in chess:

> O Edain, will you come with me,
> To a splendid castle that is mine?
> White are the teeth there, black the brows,
> And crimson as mead the lips of lovers.
>
> O woman, if you come to my proud people,
> A golden crown will circle your head.
> You shall dwell by the sweet streams of my land,
> And drink mead and wine in the arms of your
> lover.

If a male of the fairyfolk stole an earth bride and the children of the alliance did not come up to fairy standards, they were brought back to earth – but replacements were stolen on the return journey. If captured mortals were returned by using incantations or spells, they retained a strangeness in their looks and in their habits.

Fairy music had a devastating effect on mortals. It left them in a state of suspended animation with a dreamy look. Little eddies of dust whirling about on the unmetalled roads or in haggards were called *shee gaoithes*. The fairies caused them as they danced. Horses sometimes shied at these and people stopped, looked away, held their breaths and recited a prayer if they noticed one.

There is a story about a woman called Mary Kelly of Moyarta in County Clare, who was caught in a 'fairy-blast' while cutting a head of cabbage. She died and the neighbours were convinced that she had been taken to nurse a fairy infant.

Lactation appeared to be difficult among fairy mothers, for there are many cases of mothers of newborn babies being taken to nurse fairy infants. They would be allowed to return each evening to feed their own but would be bearing a dark countenance, hissing and spitting. They had to be sprinkled with holy water before being allowed back into the house. A woman who had lately given birth often began to 'act queer' and a test had to be carried out to ascertain if she had been 'replaced' by the fairies. Oatmeal was placed in some utensil and a prayer was recited. A cloth was wound around the utensil and it was placed against the woman's abdomen, sides, back and over the heart. The cloth was then taken off and the contents examined. If a fairy was present half the oatmeal would have disappeared. To remedy things, three small cakes were made from the oatmeal remaining and the woman had to eat one for the next three mornings while fasting the rest of the time.

One school of thought claimed that fairies were fallen angels going through their purgatory and that they would be raised up on the Last Day.

Most of the green hills of Ireland have their very own fairies, but those in the north-east have what amounts to a travel brochure in verse to outline their favourite tour:

Around Knock Greine and Knocknara,
Ben Bulben and Keis Corainn,
To Ben Echlann and Loch Da Ean,
North-east, then, to Sliabh Guilin,
They travel the lofty Hills of Mourne,
Round high Sliabh Donard and Ballachanery,
Down to Dundrim, Dundrum and Dunardalay,
Right forward to Knock na Feadala.

The four-leafed clover was a useful plant in fairy crime detection. An Enniscorthy illusionist had a fair-day assembly mesmerised at the sight of his game-cock strutting along the roof of a house with a huge log of timber in its beak – until a young girl asked what they were amazed about since the cock was carrying nothing but straw.

The illusionist noticed that the girl was carrying a sop of grass and asked her what she would swap it for. She asked for some fresh fodder for her horse. When she received that and handed over her own sop of grass, she ducked low and screamed that they would all be killed if the cock on the roof dropped the big log. She didn't know what the illusionist knew – that her sop of grass contained a four-leafed clover. It had prevented her from being deceived in the first instance.

But let not the Wexford people take offence at this story. We meet the same illusionist in

Kerry – the only difference in the story being that the Dingleman asked for one and sixpence for his sop of grass.

Fairies had their greatest powers in November and a red-haired man, suspect on earth, could assist a mortal in the fairy world. Many considered that 'they' were spirits not evil enough to be sent to Hell and not good enough to enter Heaven.

3

SEA AND WATER

The full impact of the ravages brought about by vulgar opulence and brash commercialism is withstood by the buttress of isolation which much of our coastline enjoys. It was in the magnificent grandeur of this isolation that I conducted a short survey of the customs and superstitions of the seafaring people. Some of these have been mentioned briefly under sections in which they became pertinent, but their very abundance and quaintness demand a separate chapter.

A man at sea may return but not a man in a churchyard. The very logic of the proverb emphasises the finality of death but also implies the very real and ever appreciated danger of the sea for those who sail her. 'A man at sea *may* return' – this is often more a hope than a certainty for the womenfolk who await the return of their loved ones: fathers, sons and sweethearts. Another version of the proverb reads: *There's hope from the mouth of the sea but not from the mouth of the grave.*

It is said that when God created the sea he appointed a king to reign over it, from whom he exacted a promise that nobody was ever to be drowned in its waters. The king did not keep his promise and he often regrets this. The trouble is that when he feels this way he causes storms, thereby continuing a vicious circle by claiming more lives.

On the Day of Judgement, the sea, fearing God, will diminish and withdraw into a cockle shell.

Fishermen do not fear the sea but they have a healthy respect for it. Women do fear it, especially when there is fog at sea. They know that their menfolk are skilled at their trade and will weather great storms, but boats have been known to be missing for days during fog, leaving womenfolk in a pitiable state of anxiety as they go about their household chores with the great burden of the possible tragedy on their minds.

When a tragedy was discovered, three days were allowed to elapse before the first funeral wail pierced the air. This was to allow the soul of the deceased some time to converse with his Maker in silence. It was also considered necessary because two huge dogs were said to sleep near the place of judgement and if awakened by wails, not even God had the power to prevent their grabbing the soul and devouring it.

May Christ and his saints stand between you and
   harm.
Mary and her Son,
Saint Patrick with his staff,
Martin with his mantle,
Brigid with her veil,
Michael with his shield,
And God over all with his strong right hand.

This old prayer invoked by fisherfolk to prevent drowning showed the place that the sea and water held in their lives.

Three boats were lashed together when leaving a harbour because it was unlucky to be the third boat out.

As on land, red-haired ladies got a raw deal and a very hostile reception was given to an auburn or chestnut beauty on board. Indeed, the mere mentioning of her name was taboo.

On the outward journey, fishermen turned their backs to the Donegal shore and prayed. When they landed in the fishing ground the fifteen decades of the rosary were recited along with the Litany of the Virgin Mary.

If a fisherman wanted a smoke and asked a crew member for a match, the full match was never given. It was split in two – not out of miserliness but to avoid giving away luck. Crew members brought along their own drinking water because, again, it was unlucky to part with some.

A knife was brought on board every ship and it was tossed into the sea if a storm arose. If other occasions for its use arose, it was stuck in the mast before being passed from one to another. At all other times it was considered unlucky to stick a knife in the mast.

A coal thrown after a fisherman as he boarded

his craft brought him luck and he always boarded from the right. Wicklow fishermen always put to sea in a sunwise direction and all fishermen like to turn a boat with the sun or to the right.

Fisherfolk considered it unlucky to keep the first salmon caught in the season, although others were not too conscientious about catching them even out of season.

Talking of salmon, it was strongly held that Mulroy Bay owed its poor salmon reputation to the fact that St Columcille was refused a salmon by a fisherman there and he took steps to punish this tightfistedness by discouraging the fish from inhabiting the bay.

St Columcille was crossing the River Finn, which separates the twin towns of Ballybofey and Stranorlar, when he slipped on one of the fine salmon that filled the river. He prayed that no salmon would ever pass further up the river than the place of the accident until a bridge was built.

Inishowen fishermen were reluctant to paint their boats green.

Along the north-west coastline some of the catch was always left on board.

A religious people, seafarers had a particularly strong devotion to the Mother of God. Fleets were blessed in most harbours and a very colourful ceremony took place annually in the Claddagh, Galway's old fishing village. Boats were adorned with bunting and the blessing of the Blessed Trinity was invoked.

Boats were similarly adorned if a fisherman married and it was customary for the groom to 'treat the fleet'. The power of a young bride over the sea was universally accepted, as this west-coast folk song indicates:

I, a virgin and widow mourn for my lover.

Never more will he kiss me on the lips;

The cold wave is his bridal bed,

The cold wave is his wedding shroud.

O love, my love, had you brought me in the boat

My spirit and my spells would have saved from harm,

For my power was strong over wind and wave.

I mentioned whistling being unlucky in the chapter on 'People' because the spirits who controlled the elements could be called up by the whistling and a storm would ensue. A new moon seen at sea, particularly if seen through glass, was unlucky.

Cleaning a boat thoroughly was said to be unlucky, as was cleaning one's sea boots before the end of the fishing season.

Granite stones were never used to weigh

down nets and nets were never loaded on an ebb tide.

Spiders on board meant good prices for catches.

If a rabbit was seen on the way to the harbour the day's fishing was cancelled.

A little harbour called Bungee in Donegal's beautiful Inishowen peninsula was said to be under the watchful care of St Buadan. It was claimed that the saint's influence was so great that no boat putting to sea from there could be lost. As a result of this belief the port was once a favourite spot for launching new craft, even if they had to be hauled great distances overland in order to do so.

Did you ever look a plaice in the mouth? An ugly-looking fellow, isn't he? Well, you see, when the herring was elected king of the sea fish the plaice grimaced in a fit of jealousy and was left that way. Another thing about plaice – it is said to be white on one side because the Child Jesus took one in his hand to ask Peter what it was called. The side that touched his hand became white and has remained so ever since.

Big shoals of herring augured well for a good harvest.

Fishermen appealed to an unfrocked priest to bring back the herring during one particularly bad season. A great number of mighty shoals returned and boats came from far-distant parts to land the fine catches. One day a number of dogfish got tangled in the nets and when plucking them out one happened to hit the priest in the face. He angrily called on the herring to get lost. The herring bonanza ceased immediately.

It was often claimed that the Devil had prevented fishermen from hauling in their nets betimes but that a good curse could send him back to hell. *Six eggs to you and half a dozen of them rotten* or *By the blessed and holy iron* were particularly effective curses, and around Clare the 'Seven Curses of Quilty' would do a very good job.

If unsalted fish were taken outdoors after nightfall by a woman, she would spend the night wandering around aimlessly until exhausted. Strange things were happened upon at times like this and one such lady saw two herrings grilling but resisted the temptation to taste the tantalising morsels. She was later told that she would never have been found had she eaten the herrings, for they were sure to be bewitched.

Off the Sligo coast lies the desolate island of Inishmurray, rich in archaeological curiosities including the famous 'Speckled Stones' (*Clocha Breaca*). When turned by an islander, they could pass his curse on to an enemy, who would die if guilty of the accusations made. Water from one of the island's wells could calm a sea if three drops were sprinkled three times to the north, south, east and west.

The island has a reputation for sanctity and the Lord himself is said to have appeared there. A forerunner of the now popular sauna is there. This 'sweat house' was used for curing ailments in joints. A turf (peat) fire was lit within. When the stones had been heated, the fuel and ashes were scraped out and the bather brought in a pallet of straw on which to lie, perspiring.

The approach to the island was treacherous and its inhabitants were often cut off from contact with the mainland for weeks. If their fires became extinguished there was a particular stone on the island which alone could reignite them.

Sea custom decreed that sharks should not be hunted on Sunday. On the morning of 25 May 1873 the crew of a boat crossing from Inishark in Clew Bay to attend Mass on the mainland saw a shoal of basking sharks. The custom was broken and a fine specimen singled out and hunted. It was harpooned but, instead of tiring, it towed its captors out to a huge wave-swept rock where the boat capsized and all on board were lost.

Some customs of the sea were peculiar. For instance, few fishermen ever learned to swim.

No family called Cregan of Kerry would ever be drowned. A Cregan went missing in a great storm and a fortnight was allowed to elapse before a wake was held in his memory. The man arrived back to join in the fun of his own wake.

Taking shortcuts from established routes near the shore was unlucky. So was sleeping in a house where an old man was married to a young woman.

A rope cannot be made from sea-sand is a fairly logical saying.

The seagull's cry is supposed to be *iasc* (fish), a likely commodity for that bird to be screaming about. A weather-rhyme about the same bird goes:

Seagull, seagull, stay near the strand,
Never good weather when you fly inland.

Seaweed which clung to the seabed was scraped and boiled in milk, and the potion drunk to clear the blood, especially if a patient suffered from boils, pimples, rashes or other dermic complaints.

Small fish found in the stomachs of larger fish were given to fever sufferers.

The oil squeezed from a cod's head was given to recently calved cows to clear them out.

Although mostly associated with the eastern part of the country, St Brigid was particularly revered along the western seaboard. Her feast day was always fine – provided a lark was heard singing at dawn. The one who heard the lark was granted good luck too.

Fisherfolk tied crosses made from straw and flowers to their doorposts on St Patrick's Day. Some killed a black cock. Once it was said that if the Palm fell with the Shamrock (i.e. if Palm Sunday and St Patrick's Day coincided) Ireland would be free. When this did occur and complete freedom was still not in sight, a rhyme emerged containing an additional requirement:

If the Palm falls with the Shamrock and the
cuckoo's in the tree,

Then and only then will this holy land be free.

On Inisheer, the tiny church of St Caomhain fills up with sands blown from the shore and it was customary on 14 June to clear the sands from the building, light candles in it and pray. A lame man was said to have been cured by following this ritual.

Tory islanders made bed-wetting children eat ashes of burned fish scales.

Greedy pollock were a sign of bad weather and even if they gobbled the bait the benefits would be only temporary, for there would be poor fishing conditions for quite a while after that.

Teelin women prayed at a well called *Tobar na Corach*, also called the 'Well of the Favourable Wind'. If it was not raining when the tide was wetting a certain sandbank, there would be no rain for a day. Teelin fishermen would never lose their nets in a dangerous sea as long as they tied a piece of *bratóg* to them. The *bratóg* was a piece of cloth from the *Bratóg Bríde* (St Brigid's cloak).

Fishermen have been jostled by unseen people believed to have been the dead, but if they carried fish no harm could come to them. They mistrusted mermaids and carried holy water to repel them, calling on them 'In the name of God, be off.' A fisherman once described seeing a mermaid, who had long golden tresses and eyes that shone like candles.

A great sea-tragedy off Inver in Donegal was said to have been caused by a witch who went through the ritual of swirling a wooden dish in a washtub of water to simulate the storm which then struck.

Changing the name of a boat was said to

change its luck and coins dropped overboard caused a storm.

Once upon a time a fisherman threw a knife at a huge wave and caused it to subside. At home that evening a strange horseman arrived and invited him to go for a ride. Reluctant to do so after his tiring day, the fisherman agreed to go out of politeness. They galloped across the sea to the opposite coast, entered a rock and came to a magnificent castle where they saw a beautiful girl with a fisherman's knife stuck in her heart. The knife was pulled out by the fisherman and the girl came alive again. Live indeed, for it transpired that she was madly in love with the fisherman and had intended sinking his ship and bringing him to her castle in the first place. She took the form of a wave to carry out her plan. The fisherman withstood her amorous advances and prevailed on the horseman to let him go back home.

As you will read in our section on death, it was considered lucky to bring a funeral across water and so an island off Donegal was a favourite burial place. Coffins were laid on a large stone slab before being brought across. On Devenish Island in Lough Erne there was a coffin-shaped stone on which people lay for various superstitious reasons.

Near relatives, long departed, were seen at times of illness in families. Sometimes they would appear out of the waves and call to fishermen at a time when some crisis was taking place on the mainland.

The pig was never referred to on board a ship or boat. Rats were considered unlucky, as were weasels.

Water in the home – not just in coastal places – had many superstitions attached to it. Water in which feet were washed was never thrown out at night. When any water was about to be thrown out, fairies were warned by the call *Huga, Huga, uisce sala.*

WELLS

Holy wells are almost as plentiful throughout Ireland as are the good people who visit them. Many wells are visited for specific purposes, most often for some cure which they have the power to offer if the pilgrim has sufficient faith. St Hugh's Well in County Westmeath, for example, is visited by sufferers from headaches. In the same field as the well there is a large stone with a hollow near its base. It is said to be the mark left by St Aedh's (Hugh's) head as he carried the stone from Killare, a good fifteen miles across country.

People cured or assisted by the intercession

of the saint associated with the holy well often left mementoes at the shrine and so it is that crutches, rosary beads, pieces of bandage and assorted rags are seen on the bushes and trees around these wells.

'Patrons' or 'patterns' were often held on the feast day of the saint after which the well was called. Some still take place and there is feasting, dancing and merry-making, sports, and *aeraíocht* or some form of entertainment in the fields around the well.

An act was passed in 1703, during the reign of Queen Anne, whereby visitors to holy wells were liable to prosecution and severe punishments. It did not kill the custom or the stories associated with these wells.

St Patrick is supposed to have stepped from Patrickswell in County Carlow to Knockpatrick in County Kildare – and his 'footprint' is in a stone there. The Carlow–Kildare area is particularly well endowed with holy wells. St Laserian was about to establish a monastery at Loram Hill, near *Muine Bheag* (Bagenalstown), when he met the dreaded red-headed woman. At the same time he heard a celestial voice which instructed him to go to where he would first see the sun shining, and build there. The place turned out to be Old Leighlin.

'Paying rounds' was an accepted ritual at many holy wells. The pilgrim walked around the well in a sunwise direction, drank its waters and scraped a cross on a stone from the well with another sharp-edged stone.

A holy well would dry up if desecrated, it was thought, but its curative powers would then be transferred to a nearby tree. People could stick pins in the tree where previously they drank the well water.

'Eye wells' cured sight loss or eye infections. Some cured sight deficiencies in animals – but at the risk of the owner becoming infected.

In some districts the hospitality of the people who lived near the well was such that few bothered to bring food or drink with them on patron day. They would be well looked after by the locals and there were always plenty of whorts (bilberries) or 'moonogues' (a speckled fruit found in marshy ground) to be picked and eaten.

Although the patterns held at holy wells had a religious significance, many of the dates coincided with the great feasts of Lughnasa, Domhnach Chrom Dhubh or Garland Sunday. These feasts took place at the end of July and the beginning of August, thus marking the end of summer and the commencement of harvest-time.

At St Brigid's Well near Moher, County Clare, people journeyed by boat from Aran to join with the mainlanders in three days of song and jollification.

All around this part of west Clare there were patterns. Lahinch had racing on the strand for their big event and people would leave the spas of Lisdoonvarna to attend. There were 'standings' aplenty – hawkers' stalls – and young and old gambled or just had fun watching 'trick-o'-the-loop men' and 'gander in the barrel' men.

Legends ignore chronology and so St Brigid is said to have been given a special feast day for having accompanied the Virgin Mary to her Purification.

Waters from holy wells were most effective during these festivals and most effective of all on the stroke of midnight separating the eve from the feast day.

Around the town of Kilcormack in Offaly there are a number of wells called after St Cormac. One day the saint was standing on top of his tower watching two snails climbing up the wall. When the snails got to the top they suddenly changed into birds and scratched his hand. Drops of blood fell on the ground as the saint went about his business and every place a drop fell a well appeared.

There was a 'curtsey stone' at Cullen Well in Cork, where pilgrims bowed their knees during the prescribed 'stations'. St Latiaran is said to have planted a whitethorn bush which grew there and it was a favourite site for faction fights between the Daithiní and the Gearaltaigh.

On Heatherberry Sunday, if the water of *Tobar na Súl* on top of Slieve Snaght in Donegal was disturbed to the extent that it became muddy, a downpour would occur – uncomfortable for the pilgrim who had to descend 2,000 feet!

Simoniacs who tried selling bottled water from holy wells have brought disaster on themselves.

Festivals were held at some wells on May Day. Many of the people attending would be young maidens in search of a man. Some dropped a mug or a bottle in the well at night and returned in the morning to see if it was floating. If so she might well receive the affections of the man she desired, but a sunken mug meant a sunken heart.

Some of the superstitions which we will discuss when we refer to milk had particular associations with holy wells at May time. Farmers who had a holy well on their land guarded it all through the night on May Eve, since his own milch cows should be the first to drink from the well on May morning to ensure good drink yields. Furthermore, it was suspected that a wandering witch scooped the top off the water to deprive the owner of its benefits if an evil neighbour requested it.

4

MILK AND FOOD

If food left out on All Hallows' Eve was gone the following morning, it had been eaten by the wandering dead.

The Sign of the Cross was made upon cakes before baking.

'Boxty', a potato bread, was a favourite christening meal. It was made by grating new, raw potatoes into a sheet, which two strong men squeezed in order to dry the potatoes. The resulting fibre was mixed into bread which was eaten hot with butter. Colcannon was a recipe with potatoes as its main ingredient. Its secondary ingredient was onion. There was a preparation known as 'sthilk' which featured mixed beans mixed into potatoes and garnished with a miscaun (roll) of country butter.

But milk and butter had the market cornered as far as superstition and custom were concerned. Giving butter away or stealing it had strict codes attached. Incantations could be uttered upon May Day which would increase the output from one's churning – to the detriment of a neighbour's. A man was getting nothing but froth from his churnings until he put the chains from his plough around the churn. He also reddened the coulter of the plough and thrust it into the milk. He heard screams and roars around the house but he got the best of butter thereafter.

'God bless the work,' said a visitor to the churner, but he had to take a hand at the churning too.

The milk of a cow that had calved was called 'beastings' and was given freely as presents, but some was always put back in the can for fear of taking the donor's luck away.

Three drops of water were always placed in milk given away.

5

PLANTS

Many hips and haws,
Many frosts and snaws.

This rhyme would have a right to its place in the section dealing with the weather, as a profusion of hips or whitethorn or holly berries denoted hardship in the weather.

Hawthorn was never brought into the house on or after May Day and the lone hawthorn was almost sacred. A whitethorn, or *sceach*, was generally regarded as unlucky.

Driving cows with a 'sally' rod would ensure a good supply of milk.

An ash with a fork or split in it was some-times used to walk a child through if it was suf-fering from whooping cough. A child was never struck with an elder switch, for its growth would be retarded by it, and 'never burn an elder' was not an appeal to youth to spare the aged.

Herbs with names like the Fairy Plant, the Mead Cailleath, the Liss More, the Fair-Gortha and others had their place in folk medicine.

The yarrow, or 'herb of the seven needs', figured prominently in superstitions. Girls dan-ced around it when they found it and sang:

Yarrow, yarrow, yarrow,
I bid thee good-morrow.

Tell me before tomorrow,
Who my true love will be.

An ivy leaf tied around a corn was said to cure it, and the milk from a dandelion was often put on warts. Dock leaves wet with spittle cured stings.

6

CURES

Folk medicine is a wide and varied subject and some herbal cures are still in use. Indeed, health shops sell cures produced from herbs, some of them based on the very folk medicine to which we refer.

A stocking filled with hot potatoes and applied to the throat cured tonsils.

A fasting spit applied to a stye in the eye for nine consecutive days would cure the ailment. The pointing of a thorn at the affected eye could also effect a cure.

Dungs of various birds, animals and insects were used for many cures and a crane buried for a month in a manure heap exuded an oil into the container that held it. The oil was useful in the treatment of burns.

A goat's bladder was sometimes filled with human urine and hung in the chimney until dry. It was then ground and rubbed into the scalp with a raw, sliced onion. It was an accepted treatment for baldness.

Mumps were feared in the countryside and an ass's winkers were sometimes worn to the well or river where the patient, still wearing the winkers, drank. A child could be cured of mumps if its head was rubbed against a pig's back while calling *muc, muc, seo dhuit do leicí* (pig, pig, here are your mumps) – but the pig would then get the disease.

A sickbed was often placed so that the head was to the north.

No disease was so serious as not to have a

remedy. Cancer was treated by blowing a herbal concoction through a quill onto the affected part. Bleeding was stopped by chewing grass blades, while cramps were relieved by the application of a 'crampstick' to the affected part. Certain families possessed the stick with the power to relieve, and its powers were much sought after. Kehoes were said to have blood which, if applied to the affected part, could cure St Anthony's Fire.

Permanent cures were a feature of the ancient health service and praying at a graveside while chewing and discarding grass plucked from the grave guaranteed a cure for toothache and immunity from further pain for a hundred years.

Hair could not be combed on Friday nor could a new moon be seen without falling on the knees to pray – even if the person was crossing a river.

Shaving on a Sunday encouraged toothache but carrying a haddock's jawbone helped prevent it.

If all that failed, a frog was caught and its two back legs were severed and soaked in water for two minutes. A spoon of pepper was then added and the lot was boiled for ten minutes. The resulting liquid was dabbed on the offending tooth.

For the benefit of that aunt with the potato, here are some genuine cures for warts. Water held for some time in a hollowed stone was collected and rubbed three times upon the wart while making the incantation: *Uisce clochgan iarraidh, ní dhot iarraidh atá mé. Ag dul abhaile a bhí mé agus casadh liom thú.* 'Water of unlooked-for stone, I was not looking for you. I was going home and happened upon you.' This water, or water from a forge where a smith cooled his irons, also cured chilblains.

Warts were often 'passed on' and if a stone was rubbed on every wart and the resulting number of stones tied in a bag and left lying on the roadway, then the finder would get the warts as they disappeared from the treated person. Warts were rubbed with a rag which was then tied to a tree to effect a cure, while self-treatment could be availed of by rubbing one's own spittle on the warts after walking.

Warts or ringworm could be cured by a man who never saw his father, if he blew three times into the patient's mouth. He would have to get some small token or gift for the service.

Seventh sons had a cure for ringworm. It was sometimes claimed that a female specimen of ringworm could be cured by a seventh daughter, but the practising of medicine by seventh daughters was rare. Ringworm or warts could be transferred to another by rubbing the affected part with raw meat and leaving it where somebody would be likely to touch it. The clay from where pallbearers walked could cure warts or ringworm too.

Stomach upsets were cured by tying a sprig of mint around the wrist, while consumption was cured by boiling mullen and drinking the juice, or by drinking ass's milk.

All ailments of the respiratory system were dreaded because of the fatal nature of consumption (tuberculosis).

Washing soda was sniffed up the nose to encourage sneezing, which could get rid of a head cold.

Bronchitis called for a rather drastic type of action. Two live pigeons or chickens were brought to the patient's bedside. One of the birds was split in two and immediately placed against the patient's chest and back. If the breathing was not considerably improved before the bird was cold, then the second bird was used in the same way.

Whooping cough often left children in great distress and there were many recommended cures for it. A stocking in which a 'hairy molly' (a furry type of worm) lay trapped was tied around the patient's neck. If the worm crawled right around the neck, the whooping cough would disappear.

Another cure for whooping cough was the passing of the child over the donkey's back to a person on the other side, who would then pass him beneath the animal's stomach. Having done this three times the child should be cured.

The treatment suggested by the rider of a grey horse was always followed in whooping cough cases, and passing the child around a donkey's head three times and then making him kiss the cross on the beast's back could bring about a cure.

Blasts (facial swellings) and felons (a type of ulceration on the finger) could be cured by an ointment resulting from the frying of lard, grass, rue, leeks and marshmallow (a weed also known as 'beggarman's cakes').

Boils could be cured by applying cuckoo-sorrel, a type of sweet weed. Boiled nettles cured boils too, and if the nettles were gathered in a churchyard they could even cure dropsy. A roasted onion cut into rings and placed upon a boil could cure it – that is, if the patient desired a cure, for I always relished the saying concerning a mean man that 'he was so mean he would grow a boil on his neck rather than buy a collar-stud'.

Before the arrival of tranquillisers, depressions were said to have been caused by a 'fairy blast' and could be treated only by pouring 'blast water' over the depressed person while praying.

Boiled daisies were dabbed on sore eyes and a more elaborate form of the treatment for a stye was also used. A sprig of gooseberry bush containing nine thorns was procured and each thorn in turn was plucked off and pointed at the sore eye. Each thorn was discarded over the left shoulder. It was said that our Saviour's crown was of nine thorns.

Tying an eel skin around a sprain assisted a cure. Boiled seaweed could help too. A very old treatment for a sprain was the winding of a strand of black wool around the affected part while saying:

> The Lord rade and the foal slade,
> He lighted and he righted;
> Set joint to joint and bone to bone,
> And sinew unto sinew.

In the name of God and the saints
Of Mary and her Son,
Let this man be healed.

If a dead man's hand was made to touch a birthmark, the mark would disappear as the buried corpse decayed.

Freckles were once treated with the spit from a hare or a bull.

A child born after the mother died was said to have the cure for thrush.

Three drops of blood were taken from the right arm of a person who had fainted in order to revive him.

There was a beautiful old prayer used for the healing of wounds which quite made up for the appalling treatment of applying fresh cow dung. The prayer, said as the wound was held closed, went something like this:

The wound was red, the cut was deep, the flesh
   was sore;
But there'll be no more blood and no more pain,
Till the Virgin Mary bears a child again.

Boiled sheep's suet and elder bark produced an ointment that could burn without leaving a scar.

Unsalted butter rubbed on a stitch in the side could cure it.

An iron ring on the finger, a copper bracelet on the wrist or a nutmeg in the pocket were said to cure rheumatism. This curse of the country people was probably occasioned by working in damp conditions and by enduring the hardships of Irish winters. It was difficult to distinguish between different forms of the ailment but the effects of the 'Fairy Darts' were very similar to arthritic conditions.

It was thought that the fairies shot their darts

at the joints causing them to become swollen. Only certain people were able to 'operate' and remove the darts. Linen taken from a corpse was said to cure swellings of this sort too. The corner of the actual linen which had wrapped the corpse was useful in the treatment of headaches. It was tied tightly around the head and the pain was said to leave the house with the dead person.

Sea produce offered many cures and the fishing folk in villages around our coasts held on to their superstitions and customs far longer than did their inland neighbours.

The fish, indeed, have their own 'doctor' and this breed of fish has, it is said, a cure in its head.

Whiting and its juice could cure a fever and eating any small fish would encourage a child's teeth to grow.

Milk in which kelp had been boiled could cure boils and clear the blood.

Small fish found in rock pools and called *craigirlín* were eaten in pairs by women as a cure for wind.

A marathon cure existed for the dreaded jaundice. A fish was caught and kept alive in a container of water until it was brought to the patient. The patient stood over the vessel containing the fish until he was exhausted. The water and the fish were then carried across the road and flung into the rising sun.

Herbal and faith cures, customs and super-stitions concerning illness were always offered with understanding and sympathy. When now-adays I hear of the sedatives and tranquillisers used to counter so many disorders, I often won-der if there was a deep philosophical message in the simple folk story about the sick woman and the borrowed shirt. This woman was ill and many cures had been tried to no avail. She was informed that if she borrowed a shirt from a woman who had no unhappiness or trouble she would be cured. She went to a woman answering the description and asked for a shirt, explaining why she chose to borrow from her. The woman called the sick one aside and told her how her godfather had been murdered by her husband for giving her a few pulls out of his pipe. He had been caught doing so by her husband and 'is buried here under the hearthstone and nobody living knows where he is … so my trouble is greater than yours, though nobody thinks so'.

7

WEATHER

Irish country people had little interest or confidence in meteorology and its talk of isobars with cold and warm fronts. My own father could foretell a wet day by the pains in his legs.

Because their harvests, and consequently their livelihood, depended so much on the weather, country people were seasoned weather prophets and whatever they could not forecast by portents, they came to grips with through superstition.

A red sky at night is the shepherd's delight,
A red sky in the morning is the shepherd's warning.

Falling soot, frogs changing colour from yellow to russet, curlews calling, midges biting, swallows flying low, spiders abroad.

> Last night the sun went pale to bed,
> The moon in halos hid her head.

Sea folk had their own signs, some mere superstitions, some with logical explanations.

The catching of the shellfish, *muireann,* on a bait was so bad a sign that boats would not put to sea for three days.

Flatfish seen on the top of the sea suggested a storm, while the little fish of the rocky pools, the *craigirlín*, if hooked, denoted a storm too.

Porpoises seen near the shore, lobster and crabs on the rocks, seagulls and other seabirds on land were all signs of rain, of storm, even of tempest.

There's no forcing the sea. The old saying may be true but the creatures of the sea appear to have some influence over its behaviour none the less. If the mackerel shone the sea would be rough and if he shone and jumped – well, fishermen could watch out!

'A Squall of Softness' was a cloud formation which indicated bad weather. A stranger to our countryside might think that a 'soft day' would be rather pleasant, but it could be anything from mildly misty to extremely wet.

8

CUSTOMS OF
DAYS AND DATES

Did you know that it was considered unlucky to go on a journey on St Martin's Eve, 10 November? On St Martin's Day, 11 November, the same held good and smallholders would be immobile, for it was also unlucky to put a horse under a cart on that day. The women would not spin either – so St Martin's Day was very unproductive in the countryside. It called for the observance of peculiar customs too. The blood of newly killed cocks would be spilled around the door-posts of houses. Rags and cloths would be soaked in the blood and stored in the rafters for they were deemed to have special properties for the control of bleeding in the event of one being wounded. In some areas the blood was sprinkled in the corners of all the rooms.

People of the Irish countryside believed that angels were always present among them and that all good things – crops, rain, dew and so forth – came from them. Bad spirits, on the other hand, brought sickness to humans and animals, and pestilence to crops. They would not speak of fairies on Wednesdays or on Fridays, for on those days 'they' could be present while still invisible. Friday was a particularly bad day. A child for a barren fairy queen, a young lady for an eligible prince, or a cow for a fairy farmer could be stolen on Friday, so it was customary to watch children and cattle closely.

The lighted coal was used for protection and

sometimes a straw was lit and wound around a baby's head.

Sick people were never visited on a Friday.

MAY DAY

May Day, when the Skelligs sailed to meet the rocks opposite and the rocks did likewise, both retiring when they had touched; May Day, when sleeping out of doors was dangerous; May Day, when the little people had a particularly detrimental effect on butter, on cream, on cows and a host of other things; May Day, on the eve of which cattle were driven into Cooey Bay from off Devenish Island to prevent their developing the dreaded cattle disease murrain.

Bunches of flowers were gathered in the fields and, apart from those that found their way through young hands to adorn the gay 'May

Bush' in family gardens, they were crushed and used to bathe the udders of cows.

Pipes were never lit from the *gríosach* (glowing red coals) of a fire on May Day, nor were embers ever taken outdoors.

Young damsels sometimes went hunting the snails in the grass on a dewy morning. 'The *drúchtín* so caught shall be placed on a plate of flour,' said the instructions, 'and the snail will move around the flour leaving in its trail the name of the one to whom the fair maid will be wed.'

Before sunrise on May morning, country people cut hazel rods out of which they carved small figures. They kept these in their stables or on their person to ward off evil.

The giving away of milk, always suspect, had further implications upon May Day, for whoever got milk of a cow first on that day received the profit from that cow for the remainder of the year. This belief was so strong that a court of law is said to have ruled in favour of a man who struck down an intruder in his byre on May Day, believing him to be after his milk.

A dying woman was refused milk on May Eve on one recorded occasion.

The much-maligned red-headed lady would not even be allowed to cross the threshold on May Day.

Dublin's southsiders had their own 'Liberty May Bush' and there was great rivalry between its people and the 'Ormond' people on the other bank of the Liffey.

CHRISTMAS

On 'Little Christmas', the feast of the Epiphany, the tail of a herring was rubbed across the eyes of a child to give it immunity against disease for the remainder of the year.

On Christmas Day itself it was most unusual for people to visit other households. This custom is still widely observed. The great feast really continued until St Brigid's Day, when the straw from the crib would be put away into the rafters as a protection against evil spirits, or as a cure for ringworm. The holly, placed around the house as decoration for the season, was usually burned under the pancakes being cooked on Shrove Tuesday, the eve of Ash Wednesday.

On Christmas Eve the youngest child in the house was brought along to where the Christmas candle was placed waiting in the window and it was a most touching moment when the little one's tender hand was guided to light the symbol of welcome for the Holy Family.

Fish was a customary Christmas Eve meal.

A special dish called *priail*, a white-sauce-coated fish, was popular.

Animals given the gift of speech, donkeys kneeling at midnight, exchanging gifts of farm produce, extra food being given to animals, mummers and 'Wren Boys' on St Stephen's Day, chimneys cleaned, all members of the family taking their turn at stirring the pudding – and turns by proxy for absent members: these were some of the customs associated with the season of Christmas before the tinsel and the paper chain, the Christmas tree and the commercial ballyhoo arrived to give us the space-saving, dehumanised 'Xmas'. But happily, the homes of many of our country people still have the beckoning candle and 'Holy Night' is not just an empty sound on disc.

On the second day after Christmas, abstaining from meat served as a preventative against fever. This precaution seems singularly attractive, for doing without meat on the second day after Christmas would be a blessed relief.

Around the Rossnowlagh area of Donegal, on the twelfth night, a ritual almost like a séance was observed. A round cake, a flat container of dried mud, sand or even animal dung was placed in the kitchen. A rush candle or a piece of bog-oak representing each member of the family was placed in the 'cake' and lit. The lights were said to have become extinguished in the order that the members of the family would die.

WHITSUNTIDE

Whitsuntide was associated with death by drowning. There were some who would not go to sea on that day unless the steady hand of a bride steered, and persons previously drowned were thought to make their return at Whit to enlist new victims for company.

Babies born then, it was said, would either kill or be killed unless a chicken was put into the infant's hand and the infant made to squeeze the little creature to death.

A foal born at Whit would either win a race or kill a man, and children often had their heads massaged with salt to prevent their being taken by the fairies.

SAINT BRIGID'S DAY

Although her cloak is said to have spanned the Curragh's vast plain when she was offered the amount of land that it would cover, St Brigid was not considered a speculator but was loved by all the Gael.

Her feast day is on the first day of February

and of spring. A doll representing the saint was carried about in some villages. This doll was called the *Brídeóg*. A churn's dash – the wooden disc on the handle that pounded the butter – was sometimes used to make the *Brídeóg*, and all the women had to bow before it as it was paraded about the village. St Brigid's Day was the feast day when crosses woven from rushes on the eve of the feast day were placed in tillage fields and in the rafters of cow byres to bring good luck on the harvest and the yields.

Children laid beds of rushes pulled by hand in front of the fire on St Brigid's Eve in case the saint wished to rest during the night. Cutting the rushes with a knife was considered wrong.

The Brigid's cross tradition is said to have originated when a golden cross commemorating the saint was stolen and the manifold weaving the humble rush type commenced to replace it.

The Irish television service, RTÉ, used the cross as its emblem during its formative years.

THE SEASON OF LENT

Shrove was the period preceding the penitential season of Lent, and Shrove Tuesday, when pancakes are made, was the day before Ash Wednesday. This was often called 'Puss Wednesday' because girls who did not manage to get a husband during Shrove would have a 'puss' on them on Ash Wednesday. It must be understood that marriages could not then take place during Lent, so if a ring wasn't tossed a girl's way along with the pancake, she had a good seven weeks to go before she could marry.

In the port of Waterford there was a custom whereby bachelors and spinsters were often tied to a large log which was dragged along the quayside on Ash Wednesday. Graffiti, often gross or obscene, appeared on the doors of their houses, and the unfortunate people suffered great embarrassments because of their single state.

Marriage was not allowed '… within the forbidden degrees of kindred or from Ash Wednesday to Trinity Sunday'. Those who didn't make it during Shrove got suitably marked on 'Chalk Sunday', which was the first Sunday in Lent. Mayo scribes did their marking on the first Monday in Lent and they took the added liberty of shaking salt on their victims.

Tying string to door knockers, climbing a roof and stuffing the chimney with a sack, taking gates off hinges and carrying them away – these were some of the pranks played on bachelors and spinsters.

Good Friday, the day of our Saviour's crucifixion, was a day when little work was done in the countryside, although in some areas it was considered a lucky day to sow potatoes. Using a hammer and nails was particularly unlucky.

On the east coast, boats in harbour would be left lying towards the quay wall on that day.

Persons who had 'given up something' for Lent watched the clock tick away the last moments of Holy Saturday as they waited to indulge once again in their abandoned luxury.

Decorated eggs boiled in water in which the blossom of furze had been stewed were rolled down hillsides on Easter Monday. A *cluideóg* (about a dozen) of eggs was a typical Easter present between country folk. Eggs and Easter were synonymous.

Blessing of stock, fields or houses with the new Easter oils was greatly sought after.

ALL HALLOWS' EVE

The thirty-first of October is called All Hallows' Eve, Hallowe'en or Hollentide. But folk customs associated with this Eve of All Saints are more concerned with All Souls (2 November). It is a time of superstition and of deep religious feelings for departed relatives and friends. It was the period when the dead were said to exact revenge for ills done to them while on this earth and when crosses were hung in their memory.

A good fire was always left burning that night – for the fairies.

People avoided taking shortcuts across beaches, fields or cliffs for fear the fairies would lead them astray.

Pairs of chestnuts left by the open fire to represent people about to be married were examined with deep anxiety, for if they stayed together on being heated then the couple would live together in harmony. But if they scattered apart there would be strife in the union.

A candle knocked over on All Hallows' Eve night was an ill omen.

Small piles of salt were often placed on a plate, each representing a member of the family. A pile that caved in signified death within the year for its owner.

If a girl sat before a mirror eating an apple she would see her future husband in the mirror at midnight.

The custom of children dressing up and going around from door to door with the 'pooka' still survives, although brash gluttony has reared its ugly head and it is not to accompany the 'pooka' but with a firm intention of gleaning as many sweets as possible from householders that children go out nowadays. The 'pooka' had various descriptions according to the part of the country, but he was usually described as a rather ugly-looking black horse.

The last night of November was said to be the closing night of the fairies' season of revelry. Better not to be out on that night for the dead have their fling of dancing with the fairies on the hillsides while drinking their wine. Thereafter they get back into their coffins until the following November.

A foolish young lady, out late on such a night, sat down to rest and was approached by a young man who invited her to tarry awhile to see the magnificent dancing on the hillside. He looked pale and sad and she soon discovered that he was a young man who had been drowned while fishing the previous June. Furthermore the dancers that he showed her were all the dead she had known.

The young man warned her to get home quickly or she would be taken by the fairies to the dance and she would never return. His advice came too late, however. The dancers arrived, encircled her and whirled about until she dropped to the ground in a faint. That she managed to get home is certain, for she was discovered next morning in her own bed, pale and gaunt, and it was pronounced that she had the 'fairy stroke'. The herb-doctor was called and every known antidote to the fairies' evil spell was employed but to no avail. The moon rose among dark clouds and slowly a quiet, plaintive music was heard without. It grew louder, the moon became clouded and the young woman slowly passed on.

SAINT JOHN'S DAY

St John's Day falls on 24 June and its eve had certain customs associated with it. Sprigs of St John's wort, a herb, were brought into homes. They were placed in windows to ward off evil, and berries from rowan trees were tied to doorposts in stables or to masts of boats.

Bonfires were lit on that night and when the bonfires would be dying down cows were often driven through. Red embers from the fire had to be tossed about in tillage fields before retiring, however. The 'Biltine' or lucky fire was really a pair of fires between which the cattle were driven to protect them against disease for the year.

In some areas young boys and girls would jump over the bonfires and the highest jumper would be the first to be married.

ODD DAYS

'Saturday's flitting, a short sitting.' In other words, nobody moved house on a Saturday, got married on a Saturday or embarked on any big project on the day before the Sabbath. Overnight travel was never undertaken.

Irish weather very often includes some very cold days at the beginning of April, just when mild, soft weather is expected. These days are said to be 'borrowed from March' and they are called *Laethanta na Riabhaí*.

The 'cold stone' was said to leave the water on St Patrick's Day, 17 March. This merely meant that milder weather was coming. Present-day resentment of Mondays stems mainly from overindulgence in the good things of modern living, but Mondays have always been out of favour among our kith. It was unlucky to break anything, especially a cup, on Monday. If salt or tobacco were given on a Monday, the week's luck would be given with it.

The first Monday of the year was known as 'Handsel Monday' and upon that day a dark-haired member of the family who had been unceremoniously instructed to leave the house just before midnight as the day approached, re-entered after the witching hour. This ensured that the dark-haired one, the harbinger of good luck, would be first into the home on Handsel Monday.

There were many occasions for refusing the incessant borrower in folklore. Although loaning was tolerated on Handsel Monday, giving away was not. If debts were paid on that day many more would be incurred throughout the year.

9

ANIMALS

A considerable proportion of the customs and superstitions of Ireland's country people are concerned with the livestock and domestic animals upon which they depend for a living. A complete book could not deal adequately with one beast alone. India's sacred cows are renowned but, although Irish bulls are famous, the milk-yielding animal's importance in the eyes of the country people has not been fully recognised. The amount of superstition and custom concerned with the cow was vast and most of it had to do with the animal's protection from evil spirits.

When a heifer had been delivered of her first calf it was customary to light a blessed candle and pass it backwards from the front of the animal and through its hind legs, burning the excess hair from around the udder in the process. This ensured that the animal's milk yield would be good.

All our fine breeds of cattle originated, folklore tells, from the three sacred cows – *Bo-Finn*, *Bo-Dhu* and *Bo-Ruadh* – brought from the sea by a beautiful maiden, Berooch. Water was used as a remedy, therefore, in any absence of issue for no apparent reason. Water from a mearin'-ditch between two parishes was the most effective.

The leg of a calf lost at birth was often kept hanging in the smoke of an open chimney to ward off the diseases known as blackleg or black quarter. Some sources claimed that the scrapings from the dried muscle of the limb were spread on threads or tapes and inserted through the skin of a healthy calf – a crude, early form of immunisation, perhaps.

The stuffing of a mixture of garlic, turpentine and glue into an incision in a cow's tail was a rather drastic treatment for worms in the tail, it seems, for there were nonchalant reports of the tail falling off the beast from the treatment.

A cure for general ailments in cattle was difficult to prepare. On Sunday night nine leaves of crowfoot were picked. They were crushed against a stone that had never been moved since the earth was created. Spittle was used (preferably early morning pre-breakfast spittle) to mix the concoction, after the usual pinch of salt was added. The resulting paste was applied to the ear of the sick cow.

St Brigid's crosses were kept in the sheds

where cows were milked and milkers made the sign of the cross on the udder with the first drops of milk.

Enmity between smallholders was comparatively rare, but a wax model of an enemy could be made to do harm to his cows. Pins were stuck in the effigy and the damage was conveyed to the livestock when the effigy was thrown into the neighbour's field.

An ivy leaf was often kept hanging over a chimney for it was believed that as the leaf dried, all soreness from cows' eyes would be taken away.

The forerunner of present-day dosing for worms was the mixing into a cow's food of a paste derived from turf, soot and salt. Near the coast, oil from a cod's head was used.

Abortion and sterility, serious ailments in cattle, could be avoided by keeping a goat in the same field as the cows.

HORSES

Horses were very susceptible to the pranks of fairies, and the fidgeting of horses in stables, so powerfully used by the playwright Peter Shaffer in *Equus* to dramatise the torture of a deranged young mind, has a much simpler explanation in folklore. The fairies, it is said, were getting free rides on the beasts. Grey horses were held in high esteem and advice from their riders was always heeded. Horses from the sea have been seen coming out to the shore on occasions of sea tragedies and a coast farmer's mare has been known to have a foal without the service of a sire.

A young wild horse was tamed by the whispering of a Creed into his left ear on a Wednesday and into his right ear on a Friday. The procedure was repeated each week until the animal was tamed.

The red-hot coal of fire, so prominent in anti-fairy warfare, was passed three times over and under a horse's body, singeing the hair in a circle around him, to eject fairies from the beast. This and other treatments for horses were often carried out when a full moon first appeared in the lunar month.

A rather cruel treatment for indigestion in horses was searing the roof of the animal's mouth with a red-hot iron.

If the finder of a horse's back tooth carried the tooth about with him he would never be short of money.

DONKEYS AND DOGS

'He'd steal the cross off an ass's back' is a reference to a thief, and the little animal that bore our Saviour along on his triumphant entry into

Jerusalem was held in respect by country men. Perhaps it was this same respect that kept the donkey comparatively free from involvement in superstition. At any rate, the use of the animal's bridle or winkers for mumps as described in our 'Cures' section is the only superstition I have come across concerning the donkey. A donkey's shoe, of course, as well as a horse's was lucky if found and nailed to the doorpost. This superstition is said to have arisen because of the donkey's presence at the Nativity.

Dogs howling near the house of a sick person were unlucky, for it was said that spirits caused the howling.

CATS AND OTHER ANIMALS

The blood of a black cat would cure St Anthony's fire and black cats were lucky. If one strayed into a home it was treated to all sorts of fancy foods to make it stay.

If a family moved house the cat was left behind. Country people were never entirely happy about where they stood with their feline friends. The cat was even denied the blessing of a visitor, who often called, 'God save all here except the cat'. It was thought that cats were extremely intelligent, possessing reason and the ability to understand human conversation.

The liver of a black cat, ground down to a powder and infused, was said to be a powerful aphrodisiac, and young maidens are said to have moved wealthy playboys to making wild love to them and propose while under the influence of cat liver!

Irish country people often tried not to look at a cat that had wiped its face with its paws. They feared seeing who the cat would spy first, for that person would be the first of the household to die.

Miscellaneous animals, wild and tame, figured in the customs and superstitions of the country people. Hares featured in numerous folktales and were often alluded to in the context of persons becoming bewitched.

A purse made from the skin of a weasel would never be empty of money, yet weasels were often regarded as old and shrivelled witches, to be feared for their spiteful and vengeful ways. To meet a weasel was unlucky and to kill one disastrous – unless one's own hen was immediately killed in reparation, prayed over and left hanging on a post in the haggard.

If the first lamb of the season was born black it was thought to indicate that black mourning clothes would be worn by the family before the year ended.

Country women would not knit until the sheep were asleep at night.

The smith was often the local vet and he administered cures to the livestock of the country people and sometimes, indeed, to the people themselves. The Irish country people were, in the main, kind to their animals and would go to great lengths to comfort or cure them.

10

BIRDS

The cuckoo comes in April,
He sings his song in May,
In the middle of June, he whistles his tune
And then he flies away.

'Hearing the cuckoo' for the first time has always carried a sort of status with it. A man would eventually settle down where he first heard the cuckoo. If he found hair on the sole of his shoe having heard it, he studied it closely, for the hair of his partner would be the same colour.

It was considered unlucky to kill a cuckoo,

but if the bird's cry was heard on one's right-hand side it was lucky.

Cows would milk blood if swallows were interfered with.

Cuttings from a person's hair were not thrown where swallows could find them for use in their nest-building, because this would leave the shorn one in danger of having severe headaches until the swallows left again.

When one did not keep tame pigeons, it was considered unlucky if a pigeon came to stay in the haggard.

A water wagtail in the vicinity of the house indicated the imminence of some bad news.

Crows flying directly over a house brought death to an inhabitant, and this bird was said to have three drops of devil's blood in it.

One for sorrow,

Two for joy,

Three for a wedding,

Four for a boy,

Five for silver,

Six for gold,

Seven for a secret never to be told.

This rhyme concerning the magpie, whose Gaelic name, *francach*, means a Frenchman, varied throughout the land and often contradicted superstitions concerning it. Position was important and while two magpies on the right-hand side brought luck for the year, three seen on one's left was an ill omen. One seemed to have been a consistent sign of bad luck.

A magpie around a door was bad luck and if it looked at somebody in the house it brought death to that person.

The red breast of a robin was received, it was

said, when the bird brushed against the crucified Christ. Robins are protected and loved because of this.

Domestic birds had their own customs and superstitions. Cocks, inheriting the stigma which their ancestor brought upon them at Haceldama, had numerous superstitions associated with their crow.

The ejaculation of 'God between us and all harm' was once used solely upon hearing the rooster's cry. If the bird faced a person as he left a doorway to set out upon a journey and if the cock crowed, the journey would be postponed. If the bird got bolder and crowed through the door or window, death would follow. A cock crowing on the doorstep heralded the arrival of a visitor.

Sean O'Casey wrote a play about a phantom cock and a comic old song about a fine cock went something like this:

This cock must have crew when they built the
    Tower of Babel,
Was reared in Noah's stable and was fed by Cain
    and Abel.
Every shot that was fired on the field of Waterloo
Wouldn't penetrate or dislocate,
This elongated, armour-plated,
Double-breasted, iron-chested,
Cock-a-doodle-do.

The female of the species had her own superstitions and a squawk from a bird 'of lay' put her in the same category as a whistling woman – unlucky. A talkative hen was likely to be brought to the nearest crossroads and let loose there after the owner had made the Sign of the Cross upon himself. The shells of hens' eggs were said to be the abodes of fairies and so it was customary to crush them after use.

The unfortunate wren, due to his betrayal of St Stephen, was hunted on the day after Christmas, killed, displayed on a bush and paraded around the countryside. The rhyme that was recited varied from place to place and this version is used to complete our few observations on birds:

The wren, the wren, the king of all birds,
On St Stephen's Day he was caught in the furze,
Although he was little, his family was great,
Rise up, landlady, and give us a 'trate'.
I whooshed her up and I whooshed her down
And I whooshed her into Robertstown.
I'll dip my head in a barrel of beer,
And I'll wish you all a Happy New Year.

11

LOVE, MARRIAGE AND INFANTHOOD

Moon, moon tell unto me,
When my true love I shall see?

What fine clothes am I to wear?
How many children will I bear?

For if my love comes not to me,
Dark and dismal my life will be.

This verse, recited by a maiden as she gathers prescribed herbs by the light of the first full moon of the new year, could reveal a future husband and could cause the girl to have a true dream about a man – if she complied with certain requirements first. With a black-handled knife she had to cut out three pieces of earth. She had to bring them home, tie them in her left stocking and secure it with the right garter. The completed package had then to be placed under the pillow upon which she was about to sleep.

Love, despite the art of the matchmaker, flourished among the boys and girls of the Irish countryside and All Hallows' Eve rings were greatly sought after, as were other signs of amorous events.

'He loves me, he loves me not' – the age-old game played as a maiden plucked the petals from a daisy until all were gone – was symbolic of the haunting question carried within most girls at some stage of their youth.

Ground hemlock, if consumed with food or

drink, could cause a man to return love. If a girl was in doubt as to whom the hemlock should be administered, she had only to throw a ball of wool into the lime kiln and wind it up until an invisible hand held it tight. If she then asked who held the wool, a voice would tell her the name of her future husband.

To ensure a lasting love, a youth brought a sprig of mint along to a meeting with his sweetheart. He held it until it became moist. He then held the girl's hand for ten minutes during which there was not a word spoken.

A strong insurance could be brought about by offering one's betrothed a drink over which the following incantation was said:

You for me and I for thee and no one else,

Your face to mine and your head turned away
    from all others.

It has never been decided, as far as I am aware, which spells or charms had the greater power, for there was one available to stir up dissension between a pair of lovers too. A handful of clay was taken from a new grave and thrown between them. The following words accompanied the throwing:

> Hate ye one another! May ye be as hateful to each other as sin is to Christ or as bread eaten without blessing is to God.

A custom still surviving is that of unmarried maidens hopping around the Metal Man, an iron monster that points to the treacherous rocks in Tramore Bay. Hopping around three times ensures marriage within the year.

That hopping reminds me that if an introduction to the 'Old Boy' himself, the Devil, is desired, it can be brought about by hopping around the Black Church at Tulla, County Clare, saying one *Our Father* backwards.

MARRIAGE

Something old, something new,
Something borrowed, something blue.

The adornments for a bride had to comply with certain recommended patterns and she never saw her groom after midnight as the wedding day was entered into. I remember being hustled away from my own betrothed on the eve of our wedding, and I also remember drinking tea in the motorcar outside the door of her home when we called before a month had elapsed from our wedding day. The bride's home was never re-entered by her or by her husband until a month had gone by. Perhaps this was a precaution against her running home to mother until she had given the marriage a fair chance!

Marry in autumn, die in spring.

This advice did not stipulate which spring, so we can only assume that it referred to the springtime of any year. As has been noted, a bride was said to have certain powers over the sea and was called upon to steer a craft in periods of danger.

She had power over fairies unless she happened to take both feet off the floor in a dance. If she did, they regained the upper hand!

Some country weddings had a beautiful custom whereby the groom presented the bride with some newly churned country butter beside a mill, a tree or a stream – all symbols of endurance. He recited a prayer that went:

Oh woman, loved by me, mayest thou
give me thy heart, thy soul and body.

There were herbal aphrodisiacs available to
married folk but, God knows, the evidence of
a soaring population seems to suggest that the
good people of the countryside needed little in
the way of encouragement for their lovemaking.

INFANTHOOD

I have seen young wives hold a cork by a string
over a pregnant friend to ascertain the sex of the
child. Older customs reflect a great underlying
fear of the power of the fairies to take away or
change an infant. An old midwife's prayer, said as
she made the Sign of the Cross on the windows
of the room where a woman was confined, bore
out this superstition:

The four Evangelists and the four Divines
God bless the moon and us where it shines.
New moon, true moon, God bless me,
God bless this house and this family.
Matthew, Mark, Luke and John,
God bless the bed that she lies on.
God bless the manger where Christ was born,
And leave joy and comfort here in the morn.
St Brigid, St Patrick and the Holy Spouse,
Keep the fairies forever from this house.

If an infant died in childbirth its mother would never have another child if the lid was nailed on its coffin.

The moment of birth had to take place when all presses in the house were open. They were immediately locked again as soon as the child was born, lest the fairies would get in and hide, awaiting their chance to steal the infant.

The Sign of the Cross was made over the infant before taking it into one's arms. This was done until the child was baptised.

A piece of metal was sewn in the child's clothes until it was baptised and no coal of fire would be taken out of the house until after the christening. Babies born at Whitsuntide were laid for a moment in a specially dug grave in order to avert disaster.

A living worm kept in the infant's hand until dead gave the child healing powers. The worm would die immediately in the hand of a seventh son.

If born in the forenoon a child would not be able to see spirits or fairies, but if born at night he could.

Water was never thrown out of the house until after a child was christened.

Difficult confinements called for the presence of a seventh son, who would shake the patient three times. If a seventh son was not readily available, any man who was not married to a red-haired woman would do. Most effective of all, however, was a drink of milk into which the black powder from six heads of blasted barley had been mixed.

On first seeing his baby, a new father kissed it five times.

12

DEATH

The popular concept of an Irish country wake relates it to an orgy of drinking, smoking and whatever other 'shenanigans' the mourners choose. The barrel of porter and the tray full of clay pipes, courtesy of the family of the deceased, were features of the most humble wake, where hospitality equalled respectability in the eyes of the neighbourhood.

But these lively wakes, for which special 'parlour games' were devised to while away the night as the corpse was 'watched', were normally held only when a person passed away in his or her old age – when death was 'normal', so to speak.

Tragic deaths were more sober affairs and 'keeners', hired professional mourners who had a piercing wail, moaned their tributes to the night air as they consoled the bereaved.

All deaths, however, had their customs to be observed. All folklore had a connection between death and water, for water was said to prevent any disquieted spirit from returning.

Happy the corpse that rain falls on,
Happy the bride that sun shines on.

Some graveyards were approached from a direction which would take the funeral over water, and if a corpse was brought to the church and the route to the cemetery passed the house of the deceased, the cortege would stop for a few moments outside the house.

Normally funerals also stopped at crossroads

and prayers were recited there. There was a strong reverence for the cross of Christ among Irish country people.

A woman's corpse buried in a men's cemetery would be ejected. An all-female graveyard in County Tyrone has its 'motto':

> No woman in it alive,
> No man in it dead.

Mounds of stones near where a man died resulted from mourners leaving a stone each. This mound was never disturbed.

If a man met a funeral he would turn back to walk a few steps with it. All blinds were pulled down in houses when funerals passed by.

If somebody stumbled at a graveside it was an unlucky sign, but not as unlucky as if he fell and touched the clay from the grave.

Persons drowned at sea were buried below the tidemark if brought ashore, but there was a certain reluctance to reclaim a body from the sea as seafarers considered that the sea might well claim another life if deprived of one.

The touch of the dead was one of the more macabre aspects of country superstition. 'Gather, gather, gather,' cried the woman of the house as she stirred the milk with the hand of the corpse. This was supposed to increase the butter yield.

If a candle was placed in a corpse's hand everybody would fall asleep. This was reputed to be a trick used by thieves' accomplices to enable a thief on the outside to come in and rob the wake-house.

Sick children were brought in for the touch of a dead hand during the day when the house was known as the 'corpse-house'. Women paid their respects during the day.

Only during the two night vigils did the house become a 'wake-house' as the menfolk took over. Before any 'celebrations' began, however, twelve candles would be lit and stood in a basin of sand. These would be replaced if necessary but would never be extinguished until the corpse was removed from the house. They would then be blown out one by one and the last one extinguished would be given to the chief mourner.

When a body was coffined, the table upon which it had lain would be upturned in order to turn death away from the family.

If the dead person's clothes were given away, the recipient had to wear them to Mass on three consecutive Sundays. If he were ill and had to miss Mass, he had to send the clothes along in a bundle.

No women were allowed in the cart that

drew a corpse to its burial, nor was a mare ever used to pull such a cart.

The gravediggers would leave their implements crossed above the open grave or four twigs would be crossed at either end of the base of the grave. When the corpse arrived it would be carried three times around the cross so made and lowered into the grave. A member of the family would throw the first bit of clay onto the coffin.

Other customs and superstitions abounded throughout the land. Pigeons have been known to accompany every funeral to certain cemeteries. It was thought that the last body interred in a graveyard looked after the other corpses until a new corpse came.

Men on white horses were unwelcome at funerals.

Shortcuts were not taken for fear of insulting the dead person.

A person who had attended a wake dipped her hands in Holy Water before handling children.

Dropping a corpse brought the most dreadful results.

Spikes were sometimes driven into a tree near cemeteries for unbaptised children when a new interment took place.

Let us relate a case history which would provide a theme for Alfred Hitchcock: A lady cut off the hand of a corpse so that she could use it at churning times. Having been buried, the corpse came to her and forced her to take the hand with her to the graveyard and beg for mercy. She was compelled to go in all weathers to the graveside for a full month and pray there for hours.

13

PLACES AND PROPHECIES

Almost every field of every county in Ireland has a particular story, a custom or a superstition associated with it. Some of these have a religious origin, others have a pagan background.

Climbers of the steep Mamore Gap in Inishowen cast a stone on a mound there, as do climbers of many mountains and hills. Stones there are aplenty that are said to have aphrodisiac powers. Stones bearing hollows have stories associated with saints kneeling on them or handling them, and a stone with a hole in it nearly always had some superstition associated with it. Expectant women passed part of their garments through one such stone at Clocnapeacaibh in Cork.

Near Cootehill in County Cavan there was a stone in the ruins of a church which exuded a type of oily substance on the first Sunday of August each year. The substance was widely used for treating ailments in cattle until a Monaghan faction carried it away after a fight with the Cavan men and it was never seen again.

Diarmuid and Gráinne must have made love all over this island if we are to take cognisance of all the large stones called 'Diarmuid and Gráinne's Bed' which adorn the countryside. Some of these are at Tulla, County Clare and Galbally, County Limerick.

Beds, chairs and other furnishings belonging to St Patrick are plentiful too, and St Kevin's

Bed in Glendalough is probably the best known of all. Custom usually called for sitting or lying in or on these.

Bold Longford children were warned of King Midas of Ardagh Hill, an ogre who might well haul them into his 'swally hole' (swallow hole).

A stone in Pulty in Leitrim was said to hold the spirit of a woman kicked into it by her cow, which she had been milking.

Livestock was protected from evil spirits by hanging a 'witch-stone' (which also had a hole through it) in the cow-shed.

A field at Ballyshane, Clonbullogue was said to yield fine crops because of the blood of a large number of 1798 rebels slaughtered in it and there are many stories of bare patches in otherwise grassy lands due to priests or soldiers being buried beneath.

In the Slieve Bloom mountains there is a

grassy patch which, if stepped upon, could cause the mountain to swallow up the intruder. A holy man is said to have cursed the spot because of a fight he saw taking place there.

Banagher in County Derry has a ruined church to which people came to scrape sand from its slabs. The sand guaranteed good luck to the possessor but not if it was passed on to another.

Clay taken from the graves of priests was sometimes given to sick people, but clay from St Mogue's island in a Cavan lake was carried by journeymen and sailors for their protection against accident or storm.

The earth had its own superstitions and an evil spell was sometimes put on a sheaf of corn which was then buried. As the sheaf rotted so would the person to whom death was wished.

An attempt to hang a Fr Kearns, a 1798 insurgent, at Bundell Wood, Edenderry, County

Offaly, failed because the rope would not function properly. An onlooker shouted, 'Soap the Rope!' This was done and the next attempt at the hanging was successful. 'Two heads are better than one,' shouted the adviser, pleased at his achievement. His family became known as 'Soap the Rope', but as a result of his exultant remark his descendants were born with two foreheads.

People who assisted at hangings were also said to have descendants who bore the mark of a rope on their necks.

If a couple involved in a turbulent marriage could be coaxed to stand on the site of a previous hanging, calm could be brought about by a neighbour stepping between them and saying:

The charm of Michael with his shield,
Of the palm branch of Christ,

Of Brigid with her veil
Be upon you.

At Teltown, Navan, County Meath, where the famous *Aonach Tailteann* (Tailteann Games) took place, there is a pond said to contain the spirit of Laoghaire, condemned to remain there until the Day of Judgement. Local people feared the spot for stock often sank in it.

Fore, County Westmeath is associated with St Feichin. There were 'Seven Wonders of Fore' and some still exist:

The monastery in a bog
The mill without a race
The water that flows uphill
The tree that has three branches
The water that never boils
The stone raised by St Feichin's prayers

The anchorite in a stone

Local superstition deems it unlucky to try to boil the water, so the authenticity of the claim may never have been tested. Branches were said to have rotted off or been broken off the three-branched tree. Every such occasion brought the same result – a new branch grew in place of the rotten or broken one.

Extollers of the lie-detector might be shocked to learn that an island in the Shannon had a black slate stone called the Cremave or Swearing Stone. The stone was a 'Revealer of Truth' and suspects were brought from near and far to swear evidence upon it. Anyone who told lies would receive facial marks that would stay with him for life and would be passed on to his issue. A hideous case history tells of a man bearing false witness at the stone. He had been accused of murder but swore his innocence, whereupon his right arm withered and his feet became paralysed. His descendants all bore the mark of a bleeding hand on their foreheads.

The fame of a Kilcoo, County Down lady called Mary Morgan spread to France, and no less a personage than Louis Pasteur, the eminent chemist who developed the pasteurisation process, called her to visit him and deal with a case of rabies. She was well known as a specialist in this field and was even called 'Mary the Bite'.

The ugly hag demanding love from a passing gentleman was a common personality on the Irish folk scene. Only the bravest responded and they were well rewarded, for at the first bit of a squeeze that old hag turned into a beautiful woman.

Inishowen had a flourishing poteen distilling industry, which neither Redcap nor Revenue

Police could stamp out. This was because the illicit distillers were given timely warning by the wee folk to whom was always thrown the first glass of the 'craythur'.

PROPHECIES

Soothsayers have not had a great image in Irish folklore, as the country people prefer the signs of nature and the elements to any man-made forebodings. But two saints have made quite an impact with their prophecies and, while their place might more rightly be in a book based on religious convictions, they are far too interesting to ignore here, for their prophecies were regarded with great respect.

The writings of St Malachi and St Columcille have captured the imagination of more than folklore enthusiasts throughout the world.

Some regard them as fakes, some respect them, but almost everybody feels a little wonderment at the uncanny construction which can be put on these writings in retrospect.

Malachi, a former bishop of Connor and primate of Ireland, was born in Armagh in 1094 and died in Clairvaux, France, in 1148. There has always been great controversy about his prophecies which relate to the popes since the time of Pope Celestine II, elected in 1143. The controversy has given way to near hysteria of late, since the saint's long list of popes is nearing an end.

After John Paul II there is only *Gloria Olivae* ('The Glory of the Olive') before '… there will reign Peter the Roman who will feed his flock among many tribulations, after which the seven-hilled city will be destroyed and the Dreadful Judge will judge his people.'

These references to the popes, of course, could be manipulated and upholders of their authenticity have delved into coats-of-arms, dates of birth, horoscopes and occurrences of a general nature to come up with a plausible explanation. For example, Pope John Paul I, who died so soon after his election, was referred to by Malachi as *De Medietae Lunae* ('of the half moon'). A full moon occurred near the middle of his short reign and so the prophecy was taken to have meant that the pope would reign from one crescent to the next.

An amusing story is told concerning an alleged incident before the conclave which elected Pope John XXIII. *Pastor et Nauta* ('Shepherd and Sailor') was Malachi's description for this pope – one which John fitted admirably having been of farming stock, having been at sea and, moreover, having occupied the See of Venice. It tells of Cardinal Spellman being interested in becoming pope and being aware of Malachi's prophecies. In order to 'qualify' he is alleged to have put some sheep aboard a boat which he hired and sailed on the Tiber.

St Columcille left Ireland in 563 for Iona, where he died in 597. His prophecies were more concerned with ancient Ireland. They generalised on the victories and defeats of the Gael and the Gall, but they contained accurate descriptions of events and ideas which have evolved since. One such account told of 'iron wheels' supporting 'fiery chariots' – and Ireland's first train ran in 1834, more than twelve centuries after the saint's death.

'An uncultivated language will be found in every person's mouth,' said Columcille. This has been accepted as referring to the decline of the native tongue.

Fr Theobald Mathew's Temperance campaign was highlighted by Columcille:

> A pure cleric without reproach will appear
> who will prohibit the use of darkened drinks.

If the events forecast by Columcille outlast those of Malachi we will do well, for he concludes:

> This new Ireland shall be Ireland the Prosperous,
> Great shall be her renown and her power;
> There shall not be on the surface of the earth
> A country found to equal this fine country.

14

MODERN TIMES

A neighbour of mine recently thought of extending her house. The house was in a built-up, urban area, had plenty of space to the rear but little at either side. Under no condition, however, would she build to the rear. That was unlucky, she claimed. This superstition probably came from the Aran Islanders' reluctance to build to the west. A family who defied this custom, some say, lost two of its menfolk to the sea and a third to the 'lunatic asylum' as the mental hospital was then called.

Money won at cards is seldom given to another player for fear of giving away the luck with it. I know of at least one household that turns a blind eye to any rumpus short of an orgy, yet will not allow cards to be played within its walls, for card-playing is the Devil's game and should not be tolerated at all.

Visitors to a house should not use the same door through which they entered the house for their departure. This custom is very much still alive in some areas.

Green is still considered to be an unlucky colour.

It is considered unlucky to open an umbrella indoors and shoes should not be placed on a chair or on a table. This and many other superstitions are still heeded by theatre folk, many of whom roamed the countryside with their 'fit-ups' in the past. They played on village green and market square within their portable palace of varieties made of canvas and wood.

But in their city dressing rooms today, many an actor believes that if a shoe falls over on its side, bad luck will follow. If a quick change necessitates kicking off the shoe and it lands upright, that is a good sign. The actor whose shoes squeak on his first entrance will be well received by his audience.

It is lucky to have a theatre cat – as long as it does not run across the stage during the performance. Cats should not be kicked by angry actors either.

Whistling in the auditorium is frowned upon, but if someone whistles in the dressing room (we saw earlier that this was unlucky) he is put outside and made to turn about three times before being admitted again.

Power failure or not, three candles are never lit on stage or in the dressing room, for a quarrel among the cast will follow such an action.

Actors and actresses will not look into a mirror over another's shoulder. Few amateur productions would ever get under way if this were observed, for often a broken piece of mirror serves for everybody.

Professionals will not call Shakespeare's play *Macbeth* by name. They refer to it as the 'Scottish play' and they tell of a remarkable history of tragedy associated with the performance of this classic.

The front of the house has its customs and superstitions as well. An elderly person buying the first ticket ensures a long run of the show, while a young customer is unwelcome. An usherette will consider herself lucky if she seats the first patron – except in seat number thirteen.

Thirteen, of course, is always considered an unlucky number, it being the number of people who sat at the table on the eve of Christ's crucifixion. Some modern hotels have no room number thirteen.

Footballers have on occasion refused to wear number thirteen on their backs, while footballers and hurlers are loath to have their photographs taken at half-time.

Many a goalkeeper casts a horseshoe into the back of the net to bring his team luck.

The 'luck penny' or the giving back of a certain amount of the cash paid is still a feature of bargain making. It is very common where fairs survive and where a deal is still settled by spitting on the palm and slapping the hand of the customer. A man's status in a neighbourhood is often determined by the size of the 'luck penny' he is in the habit of giving.

In some families a silver coin is left under the pillow of a little one who has lost a baby tooth. It is supposed to be a gift from the fairies.

If a young woman is served tea and there are two spoons on her saucer, that is the sign of an approaching christening.

In Connemara, the word *prinkum* is sometimes used for a *ceilí* or house party. It was once used for a 'Cake Dance', which was a feature of folk life in Roscommon and Meath, even if its form varied from place to place. It was a type of ritual dance in which a decorated cake was used. Decoration on homemade soda bread – little squiggles of the left-over dough – are still quite common, as is the Sign of the Cross cut on the cake, a custom that unwittingly aids the division of the cake too.

The dances were held mainly at crossroads or near a drinking house. A boy and girl, often called the 'hurling couple', led one particular dance and collected monies for the musicians as they danced.

Ordinary crossroads dances are well remembered, of course, and Kilkenny people still talk about 'the boords of Ballycallen'. They talk – and remember.

Even in the over-crowded emptiness that is modern living, the countryside and its ways are remembered – for few families are metropolitan through and through. When next you look through the uncurtained windows of the nouveau riche and see their opulence on display, sympathise rather than condemn, pity rather than envy.

CONCLUSION

In this brief discourse on the customs and superstitions of Irish country people, I have tried to present the mere bones of the story. Examples quoted come from sources written, spoken or seen, and from blurred corners of a memory which once held an abundance of the lore of the countryside. If the reader wishes to put flesh on the bones and if this book has prompted him to do so, then it has achieved its objective. There is a vast area to be covered, but thanks to worthy people who have given of their time, energy and patience, there is a wealth of information available to intending students or to anyone just interested in the quaint, gentle and altogether fetching ways of a wonderful people.

For those who have read this far only to discover the fate of my wart, let me say that I have written to an eminent archaeologist inviting him to examine it with a view to carrying out a dig.